W9-AET-798

Ye Yucky MIDDLE AGES

THERE'S A RAT IN MY SOUP

Could You Survive Medieval Food?

Chana Stiefel
Illustrated by Gerald Kelley

Enslow Publishers, Inc.
40 Industrial Road
Box 398
Berkeley Heights, NJ 07922
USA

http://www.enslow.com

Library of Congress Cataloging-in-Publication Data

Stiefel, Chana, 1968–
    There's a rat in my soup : could you survive medieval food? / by Chana Stiefel.
        p. cm. — (Ye yucky Middle Ages)
    Includes index.
    ISBN 978-0-7660-3785-4
    1. Food habits—Europe—History—To 1500—Juvenile literature. 2. Cookery,
Medieval—Juvenile literature. I. Title.
    GT2853.E85S74 2011
    394.1'2094—dc22   2010020757

Paperback ISBN 978-1-59845-375-1

Printed in the United States of America

042012 Lake Book Manufacturing, Inc., Melrose Park, IL

10 9 8 7 6 5 4 3 2

To Our Readers: We have done our best to make sure all Internet Addresses in this book were active
and appropriate when we went to press. However, the author and the publisher have no control over and
assume no liability for the material available on those Internet sites or on other Web sites they may link
to. Any comments or suggestions can be sent by e-mail to comments@enslow.com or to the address on
the back cover.

Illustration Credits: © 2010 Gerald Kelley, www.geraldkelley.com

Cover Illustration: © 2010 Gerald Kelley, www.geraldkelley.com

Contents

CHAPTER 1
Freaky Feasts *page 5*

CHAPTER 2
The Royal Table *page 12*

CHAPTER 3
Gruel Again?! *page 30*

CHAPTER 4
Empty Bellies *page 38*

Words to Know *page 44*
Further Reading *page 46*
Internet Addresses *page 47*
Index *page 48*

Freaky Feasts

Turning a long metal skewer, the cook roasts a whole swan over a blazing fire. For gravy, he mixes the bird's blood with its heart, liver, and guts. He stirs in pieces of bread and adds some broth. The swan's skin and feathers are then stuck back onto its body to make it look alive. Dinner is served!

Is this the latest edition of some gross-out cooking show? Nope, it's a thousand-year-old recipe from the Middle Ages. This was a period from about the year 500 to 1500. The Middle Ages were wild times. Everyone—rich or poor—worried about war, disease, and starvation. During times of peace, rich **nobles** hosted fabulous (or freaky) feasts in castles all over Europe. They served a parade of jaw-dropping dishes. Meanwhile, poor peasants who worked the fields ate lumpy porridge.

Food trends change with the times. What we might call "yucky" today, people in the Middle Ages called "dinner." For a taste of mealtime in the Middle Ages, dig in!

Creature Features

A big feast in a medieval castle was a spectacular event. The rich lord of a castle loved to surprise his guests with crazy cooking creations. Pigeons, eagles, and crows—birds you would never imagine eating today—were cooked into

fancy dishes. Sometimes small birds, such as hummingbirds and doves, were stuffed into larger birds. Peacocks were served with their colorful feathers on full display. Of course, it wasn't just birds on the menu. It was a multi-course food marathon.

No animal parts were wasted. People enjoyed eating animal livers, brains, hearts, lungs, necks, feet, and behinds. They even ate cows' udders! Animal intestines were used as wrappings for sausages. Bone marrow (the soft tissue inside bones) was mixed into pies and tarts. As with the roasted swan, even blood was used as an ingredient in sauces, gravies, and stuffing. Fish, fowl, and meat were stewed in a mixture of half blood, half broth. And you didn't have to be a vampire to eat it!

To create a "creature feature" that resembled a hedgehog, a pig's stomach would be stuffed with ground pork, ginger, nuts, and spices. The outside would be decorated with almonds to look like the animal's spines. For a real shocker, some cooks would sew the head of a rooster onto the body of a baby pig—or the other way around! Boiled calves' feet were used to make gloppy **gelatin**. This is not the sweet Jell-O® people are used to eating today. These wiggly jellies were dyed blue to look like the sea. Whole cooked fish would "swim" in them.

Louis the Fat

Gluttony, or "pigging out," is thought to be a sin. Yet medieval feasts still led to overeating. King Louis VI of France was so large he became known as "Louis the Fat." He reigned from 1108 to 1137. According to legend, Louis was so big he had to be lifted onto his horse with a crane.

Gone Fishing!

Wednesdays, Fridays, Saturdays, and the forty days before Easter were considered fasting days in the Middle Ages. Catholics could not eat meat. Instead, they ate fish. Sometimes cooks would mash up the fish and shape it to look like meat. For example, pink salmon and white pike were used to make fake ham.

Surprisingly, since beaver tails were considered fishlike, people were allowed to eat them during a fast. Because these furry mammals were so popular for their fur and meat, they were nearly wiped out in Europe. Whale meat was a rare fast-day treat fit for kings and queens. Other unusual seafood included porpoises, seals, and walruses. Rabbits and frogs also were gobbled up on fast days.

Eel-like creatures called **lampreys** could be found

Colorful Cooking

Do you like green eggs and ham?
Apparently, people in the Middle Ages did!
Foods were dyed a rainbow of colors. Pork
and other meats were dyed green with
leeks, spinach, or parsley. Sometimes the
green meat was rolled into big meatballs
to look like apples. Fish eggs were painted
green with pea juice. Roasted cranes were
tinted gold with egg yolk, dandelions,
and a yellow spice called saffron. A plant
called draco, or dragon's blood, turned
food blood red. Crushed violets dyed food
purple. Diners guzzled it all down.

in many popular dishes. These long, slippery creatures have tooth-lined sucking mouths. They suck the blood of larger fish. In England it was a tradition to present the king with a lamprey pie every Christmas. In 1135, after a long day of hunting, King Henry I of England sat down to a lip-smacking meal of lampreys. A doctor had warned him to lay off the eels. Nevertheless, Henry stuffed himself so much that he became sick. The next day, he died from a "surfeit [overload] of lampreys."

If fresh fish wasn't available, people ate smoked, dried, or salted fish. Salted herring was eaten by the barrelful. Many people grew sick of herring. One medieval boy lodged a fishy complaint. See if you can decode his Middle English:

"Thou wyll not beleve how wery I am off fyshe, and how moch I desir that flesh [meat] were cum in ageyn [again], for I have ate non other but salt fysh this Lent, and it hath engendryde [engendered] so moch flewme [phlegm] within me that it stoppith my pyps [pipes] that I can unneth [neither] speke nother brethe."

2

The Royal Table

Breakfast time was at dawn. Forget waffles and pancakes. The first meal of the day typically was bread soaked in wine. The main meal of the day—dinner—was eaten in the late morning. A light supper was served around 5 P.M.

Sometimes, mealtime at a castle was full of entertainment. Imagine having a circus in your kitchen or dining room! Jugglers or acrobats would surprise guests by jumping out of giant puddings. Musicians might leap out of huge castles sculpted from pastry dough. Marzipan, a sweet paste made of almonds, sugar, and eggs, was used to create statues of saints, ships, wild beasts, or fire-breathing dragons.

The Great Hall

Meals were served in the castle's **Great Hall**. This was a large room with a high ceiling. At night, servants and staff slept in this room. During the day, tables were set up for meals. One long table was set on a platform, higher than the rest. This was reserved for the lord and lady of the castle and their most important guests. The lord could look down on the other tables. It was considered a great honor to sit near the host. Sometimes fistfights broke out over the seating plan.

The tables were spread with white cloths. Most people sat on benches, picnic style. Guests received spoons for soup, dishes for salt, drinking cups, and shallow wooden bowls called **mazers**. Visitors brought their own knives, tucked into their belts. Most people sliced their meat with a knife. Then they ate with their fingers. Forks weren't used until the 1460s. So people were careful to wash their dirty hands before and after eating.

13

Two people shared a dish, but they did not eat off plates. Sometimes they put their food on a stale piece of flat, dry bread called a **trencher**. The trencher would soak up gravy and grease. Trenchers didn't go to waste. Soggy used trenchers were handed out to poor, hungry beggars who stood at the gates of castles.

You might think of people in the Middle Ages as being rude or crude. Yet castle dwellers and their guests had very good manners. The mess under their tables, however, was a different story. It was worse than a cafeteria after a food fight. Under the feet of diners, the floors were covered with spilled

Mind Your Manners

Here's how to mind your manners the medieval way: Go to the toilet before eating to avoid passing gas at the table. Avoid picking your teeth, fingernails, or nose. Don't feed cats or dogs during the meal. Wipe your mouth before drinking. Keep your hands and nails clean. Don't stuff your mouth. Avoid cursing or talking about unpleasant topics, such as disease. Don't belch.

beer, grease, bones, spit, and poop from the dogs, cats, and rats that ran free around the castle. Large woven mats or straw were used to cover the mess. Sweet-smelling herbs, such as lavender and mint, had to be tossed in with the straw to mask the nasty smells.

Drinking Problem

Rivers and streams in the Middle Ages were used as a town's water supply. However, they were also used as the sewer! That means that human waste, garbage, and food scraps were often dumped into rivers. In the 1300s, the Thames River in London was filled with some of the yuckiest stuff imaginable: human poop, animal guts, dung, blood, drowned puppies and cats, and dead fish. Oozing mud was so thick that ships could barely pass through.

As you can imagine, the water was terribly polluted. Unless people lived near a clean spring, they usually avoided drinking water. They didn't know about harmful germs, but they did know that dirty water caused cramps and diarrhea. Drinking polluted water also led to a number of deadly diseases, including **dysentery**. The symptoms of dysentery include bloody diarrhea, fever, severe stomach cramps, and bloody vomit. Rich and poor people alike suffered from dysentery. Many medieval kings died from this nasty disease.

So what did people drink? The main drinks were wine and a watered-down beer called **ale**. Alcohol killed some of the bad germs in the water. Wine was made in huge vats.

17

Workers sometimes stomped on squishy grapes with their bare feet. Grapes were also crushed in a hand-cranked machine called a wine press. The castle bought wine by the barrel. It was poured into jugs. Because there were no corks, there was no way to keep germs out. Wine often turned to sour vinegar with thick gunk floating in it. A butler sometimes added spices, such as ginger or cinnamon, to make the wine taste better. This is how Peter of Blois, a French poet, once described the vile wine served in the court of King Henry II:

"The wine is turned sour or mouldy—thick, greasy, stale, flat and smacking of pitch [tar]. I have sometimes seen even great lords served with wine so muddy that a man must needs close his eyes and clench his teeth, wry-mouthed and shuddering, and filtering the stuff rather than drinking."

Kings and other nobles often worried that their enemies would try to kill them by poisoning their wine. A butler would often taste the noble's wine first! This was one of the dangers of the job. It was also a sign of loyalty and trust.

18

Peter of Blois also described ale or beer as "horrid to the taste." This alcoholic drink was brewed by women called alewives. Ale was made from boiled barley, wheat, and oats. Mostly servants and peasants drank ale. Flowering herbs called **hops** were added to the ale to give it a bitter, tangy taste. Like alcohol, hops killed germs in the ale.

The Castle Cook

Castle cooks sometimes got a bad rap. They had a messy, noisy, and smelly job. Cooks were in charge of many workers. In the kitchen, young boys turned whole dead animals on a spit over an open fire. Smoke filled the air. Tempers flared. Sometimes cooks would beat the boys with their large soup ladles. They also chased away the rats, cats, dogs, and flies that zipped through the kitchen.

Blackbird Pie

Do you remember this nursery rhyme?

> Sing a song of sixpence,
> A pocket full of rye;
> Four-and-twenty blackbirds
> Baked in a pie!
>
> When the pie was opened,
> The birds began to sing;
> Wasn't that a dainty dish to set before
> the king?

At medieval feasts, cooks would actually place live birds between baked piecrusts. When the king or lord of the castle cut into the crust, the birds would fly free.

Some cooks had a sharp sense of humor. They would serve live animals as a practical joke. For example, they would dish out a bowl of squirming live lampreys. Or they would paint a live brown lobster red and place it on a platter with cooked lobsters. When a server would reach for the platter, the live lobster would snap at him with its claws!

Today some of these animal antics would be considered abuse. For example, the cook would plunge a live chicken into hot water and pluck its feathers. Then he would paint the naked bird brown so it looked roasted. He would spin the bird around until it was so dizzy it would stop moving. The stunned chicken was placed on a platter and served with roasted meat. When it was time for carving, the chicken would wake up and bolt across the table. Guests would shriek as the squawking chicken turned over jugs and bowls.

Guests or kitchen staff would sometimes try to get back at the cook. They would sprinkle the dried blood of a lamb or rabbit onto meat to make it look bloody. Or they might put stringy animal guts on a plate of fish and scream, "Worms!" In one story, someone snuck into the kitchen and put soap in the stew. The pot bubbled over nonstop.

Getting Ready for Winter

Practical jokes aside, cooks had to put up with many real-life challenges. They worried constantly about stocking the castle kitchen. Ye Giant Supermarket didn't exist in the Middle Ages. There were no trains, trucks, or planes to deliver food from faraway places. Most food came from farming, hunting, or slaughtering animals. Cows, pigs, and sheep hung out near the kitchen until the cook was ready to kill them. Food also was bought at outdoor markets. Some merchants would try to sell spoiled meat after sundown because customers couldn't see that it was rotten. Laws were passed so meat could not be sold by candlelight.

25

Stinky Myth

Here's a stinky myth about castle meat: People used to think that as meat rotted throughout winter, the castle cook would add more spices to cover the nasty smell and flavor. The truth is, if people had eaten rotten meat, they would have gotten sick or died from food poisoning. People in the Middle Ages didn't know about bacteria, but they could taste and smell spoiled food. They would have known that eating rotten meat would make you sick. Cooks added spices to meat for the same reason we do: to add a flavorful "zing."

Winter posed a major challenge. There were no refrigerators or freezers to keep food fresh. After a few days or weeks, most fresh fruits and vegetables would get mushy or turn moldy. Some produce, like peas or beans, could be dried. The winter menu was slim.

Fresh meat was a bigger problem. During winter, there wasn't enough hay or grass to feed livestock. In rich households, November was nicknamed "blood month." In November, pigs were fed acorns so they would fatten up. Then the pigs—and other farm animals—were slaughtered. Only the youngest and best animals were kept alive for breeding.

Medieval Recipe: Brawn Royal

Chop up pork with the meat of a wild boar. Stir it with spices and a blend of mashed almonds simmered in milk. Cook the concoction in a pot until it thickens. Next, pour the mixture into a linen cloth, roll it into a log, and let it cool. Once unwrapped, the meat will form a sausage. Cut thick slices and arrange them on a dish. Paint the slices green with ground leeks, brown with cinnamon and ginger, and purple with crushed violets. Surround the colored meat with the ribs of the pig and boar so they create a "rib cage." Serve and enjoy!

From tongue to tail, almost all parts of a pig were cut up.
People would eat a pig's ears, snout, liver, stomach, bladder,
intestines, and feet. The animal's fat was used for cooking. Its
gallbladder was used as medicine.

Medieval people had a few ways to preserve meat and
fish for winter. In some parts of northern Europe and Asia,
the long, freezing winters meant that meat could be frozen in
ice. In the 1400s, an Italian ambassador visited an outdoor
market in Moscow, Russia. The market was held on the city's
frozen river. The ambassador was amazed to see whole cows
and pigs—without their skin—standing upright, frozen solid.

They were like frozen meat sculptures. The animals had been slaughtered at least three months earlier.

In most of Europe, meat and fish were soaked in a salty solution called **brine**. Brine helped preserve the meat. Another way to preserve meat was to bury it in a bed of dry salt. Sometimes the meat was smoked. These methods worked because they drew out the meat's oil and water—substances that harmful germs and mold like to grow in. Another way to preserve meat was to smother it in animal fat or gelatin. First the meat was cooked. Then it was covered with gelatin made from boiled calves' hooves or in globs of animal fat. The meat was stored in crocks or sealed containers in a cool place, such as a cellar.

Gruel Again?!

A peasant's diet was a far cry from the fancy food of the wealthy class. Peasants farmed the nobles' land. They sometimes grew their own crops, too, such as cabbage, peas, beans, onions, turnips. A peasant's main food was a pasty dish called **pottage**. A peasant's pottage was made with boiled peas or grains such as oats. It might stew over a fire for days. Sometimes they threw bones, root vegetables, onions, or apple cores into the pot. Rich people ate pottage too, but theirs was a thick, meaty stew.

Beef was very expensive. For protein, poor people mainly ate pork, fish, cheese, and eggs. Peasants could not hunt for big animals, such as deer, wild boar, or bears. Hunting was an expensive sport reserved for rich nobles. Peasants couldn't afford the horses, spears, and swords

Royal Stomachache

While the poor were scrounging for food, rich people threw massive feasts. In 1465, a huge feast was prepared for 6,000 people at Cawood Castle in England. The shopping menu looked something like this:

Ye Shopping List

104 oxen

6 wilde bulls

1000 sheep

304 calves

400 swans

5000 geese

100 capons

3000 pigs

104 peacocks

13000 various birds

504 stags

1500 pies

600 fish

12 porpoises/seals

13000 sweet meats

1 large antacid

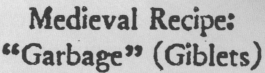

Medieval Recipe: "Garbage" (Giblets)

Rinse chicken "garbage" giblets, such as heads, feet, livers, and guts. Throw them in a pot and add fresh beef broth. Sprinkle with pepper, cinnamon, cloves, mace, parsley, and chopped sage. Add bread and steep it in the broth. Draw it through a strainer. Add powdered ginger, verjuice (sour grape or apple juice), salt, and a little saffron. Then serve!

needed for hunting. Nobles often owned the land and forests where they hunted. Hunting illegally is called poaching. If a poor peasant was caught poaching, he was either put to death or his hands might be chopped off!

Bread Basics

Bread was a staple of the medieval diet. People paid high fees to grind their grain into flour at a mill. Millers often cheated people. They put their thumbs on the scale to make grain seem to weigh more. That meant people had to pay more.

In addition, most people did not have ovens in their homes. Wood for fires was costly. So people carried their dough to public ovens for baking. They had to pay to use these ovens.

Many bakers were known to be cheaters, too. They stole bits of dough from the townspeople. Then they would bake bread and sell it for profit. Sometimes they added dirt, sand, ashes, or cobwebs to the dough to bulk it up. They also filled meat pies with nasty, tossed-out animal parts. A baker who was caught cheating would be punished. He was dragged through town on a sled with a loaf of bread tied around his neck.

In the Middle Ages, even bread was a status symbol. The best quality bread was called **wastel**. It was made from white flour. Only rich nobles—and their dogs!—were lucky enough to eat wastel. **Manchet** was another kind of high-quality bread. It was made from ground wheat. Manchet was sweetened with rose water, nutmeg, and cinnamon.

Common people and poor peasants ate hard, coarse bread. It was made from oats, barley, and rye. During the Middle Ages, the heavy use of rye led to a very bizarre disease called **ergotism**. Ergot is a black fungus that grows on wet grain. Following wet summers, ergot would grow out of control on rye crops. When people ate rye bread tainted by ergot, they developed some wacky and painful symptoms. People felt like their limbs were on fire. Their hands and feet turned black like coal. Sometimes people's fingers, hands, and toes had to be cut off to prevent the spread of infection. People sickened by ergot vomited and had seizures (severe shaking episodes). People would go mad and dance crazily in the streets. Many people died. Ergotism is also called "Saint Anthony's Fire." It was named for a hospital in France dedicated to Saint Anthony. The monks there cared for victims of ergotism.

Crayfish Ash and Goose Fat: Foods that Cure

Feeling ill? "Medicine" in the Middle Ages sometimes came from food. Check out these yucky "cures."

❖ Got an earache? Goose fat would be dripped into your ear!

❖ A drink made with the ground-up horn of a male deer was thought to strengthen the heart and chase away worms.

❖ Roasted turtle doves were eaten to sharpen memory.

❖ Ashes from the burned shell of a crayfish, mixed with ground purple flowers, were thought to cure infections from dog bites.

❖ Fresh butter was slathered on the sore gums of teething babies.

Puffy Gums and Tooth Worms

In winter, because there were fewer fruits, many people suffered from **scurvy**. This is a disease caused by a lack of vitamin C. The symptoms include puffy gums and blotchy skin. People also got sick with cramps and diarrhea when they gorged themselves on fresh fruits and vegetables in the spring.

Chewing on coarse bread and eating sweets also led to toothaches. People didn't have toothbrushes or toothpaste. They picked food from their teeth. Dental care involved gargling with wine or vinegar and scrubbing teeth with a towel. People gnawed on reedy plants that grew near marshes. After a meal, they would chew on spiced candies, anise, fennel seeds, mint leaves, or other herbs to freshen their breath. Still, without proper dental care, teeth must have been terribly rotten. People believed that cavities were caused by "tooth worms" burrowing holes in their teeth and gums. There were no dentists. Barbers (the "surgeons" of the Middle Ages) or traveling tooth pullers would yank out rotten teeth. They sometimes poured acid on the infected area. That killed the nerves and dulled the pain.

37

4

Empty Bellies

Throughout the Middle Ages, people stressed about the possibility of starving to death. Peasants worked hard to grow good crops. If crops failed, people could go hungry. Of course, no one could control the weather. As any farmer knows, too much rain—or too little—can destroy crops. Too much rain would flood the fields or make grain and other crops moldy. Too little rain would make crops shrivel up and die. People constantly worried about whether they had enough food stored. Famine was common in the Middle Ages.

In the spring and summer of 1315, cold rain drenched fields all over northern Europe. Harvests were far smaller than usual. People used up their stored supplies. They gathered whatever edible roots, plants, grasses, bark, and nuts they could find in forests. Everyone—rich and poor—suffered.

More heavy rains fell in 1316. People began to starve. Animals died from lack of food and from disease. People ate dogs, cats, and horses. There were horrifying rumors of people eating other people. By the summer of 1317, the weather had returned to normal. Yet people were too weak to recover quickly. They suffered from diseases. There was little grain left to use for seed. The death toll of the Great Famine of

1315–1317 isn't known. By some estimates, 7 million people—or 10 percent of the European population—died of starvation. The food supply didn't return to normal until about 1325.

Starving in a Siege

Aside from famine, one of the biggest threats to a castle was a siege. An attacking army would surround a castle and cut off its food and water supply. They would try to starve the residents until they surrendered. Sometimes a kind lord would protect peasants or villagers in his castle. Many castles were prepared for a siege. They might store a year's supply of food. As the enemy approached, they would bring in cows, sheep, and other livestock.

In 1095, thousands of German and Italian soldiers took over a fortress called Xerigordon near Nicaea, in what is now Turkey. The Turks tried to reclaim their fortress. They blocked the castle's water supply. The castle's defenders nearly died of thirst. Some people drank horse blood. They even drank each other's pee! People buried themselves in damp soil. They thought they could absorb moisture through their skin. Finally, after eight parched days, the castle gave up. Many of the surviving troops were either killed or sold as slaves.

Lessons from a Medieval Cook

Would you eat snakes, snails, or an octopus? Could you gobble down a grasshopper? How about dog or shark meat? These aren't disgusting dishes from the Middle Ages. They're foods eaten *today* in different parts of the world. Sometimes people depend on whatever foods are available. Other times, it's a matter of taste.

41

Without a doubt, many foods of the Middle Ages would make you gag. Yet you have to give medieval cooks some credit. They struggled through terrible times of famine and siege. They were very creative with the food that was available. During times of peace, castle cooks managed to put together huge feasts without the luxury of giant supermarkets. They didn't even have a refrigerator to keep food fresh. There were no stoves for cooking.

Like medieval cooks, many chefs today try to wow their guests with wild recipes. Some dishes from the Middle Ages have even made a comeback. Have you ever heard of haggis? In this recipe, a sheep's heart, liver, and lungs are mashed together with onions, oatmeal, and spices. All these ingredients are stuffed into the animal's stomach and simmered. The original recipe appeared around 1430. Today, it's the national dish of Scotland. It's prepared or sold in gourmet markets around the world. You can even buy haggis in a can. How's that for a taste of the Middle Ages?

43

Words to Know

ale—A weak beer.

brine—A salty solution used to preserve meat.

dysentery—A deadly disease sometimes spread by polluted drinking water; symptoms include bloody diarrhea, fever, and vomiting.

ergot—A black fungus that grows on wet grain. It caused a painful and deadly disease called ergotism, also known as St. Anthony's Fire.

gelatin—A jellied food that is made from boiled animal bones, such as calves' hooves.

Great Hall—A large room in a castle in which meals were served and staff slept.

hops—A flowering plant. The flowers are added to ale to give it a bitter, tangy taste.

lamprey—An eel-like creature.

manchet—High-quality bread made from ground wheat.

mazer—A type of small, shallow bowl.

noble—A wealthy man who owned land.

pottage—A type of thick soup or stew that was the main food for most people in the Middle Ages.

scurvy—A disease caused by a lack of vitamin C.

trencher—A type of flat, dry bread that was used as a plate.

wastel—Good quality bread made from white flour.

Further Reading

Bhote, Tehmina. **Medieval Feasts and Banquets.** New York: The Rosen Publishing Group, 2004.

Elliott, Lynne. Food and Feasts in the Middle Ages. New York: Crabtree Publishing, 2004.

Gravett, Christopher. Eyewitness Castle. New York: Dorling Kindersley, 2004.

Hunt, Norman Bancroft. **Living in the Middle Ages.** New York: Chelsea House Publishers, 2009.

Internet Addresses

The British Library Board:
Books for Cooks/Medieval Food
**http://www.bl.uk/learning/langlit/booksforcooks/
med/medievalfood.html**

James L. Matterer.
"A Boke of Gode Cookery."
http://www.godecookery.com/godeboke/godeboke.htm

Index

A
ale, 17, 19

B
barber surgeons, 36
blackbird pie, 21
brawn royal, 27
bread, 5, 12, 14, 32–34, 36
    manchet, 34
    wastel, 34
breakfast, 12

C
castles, 5, 6, 12–14, 16, 18, 20, 24, 26, 31, 40, 42
Christmas, 11
cooks, 5, 7, 9, 20, 22–24, 26, 27, 42
    jokes, 22–24

D
dining tables, 13–15, 23
dinner, 6, 12
dyed food, 7, 10
dysentery, 17

F
famine, 38–40, 42
fasting, 9

feasts, 5, 6, 8, 21, 31, 42
    entertainment, 12
    menu, 6–7, 31
fish, 7, 9, 10, 11, 17, 24, 28, 29, 30, 31
food sources
    farming, 24, 30, 38
    hunting, 11, 24, 30, 32
    livestock, 24, 25, 27
    markets, 24, 28, 42

G
gelatin, 7, 29
germs, 17, 18, 19, 29
giblets, 32
Great Hall, 13

H
haggis, 42
Henry I, 11
Henry II, 18
hops, 19

L
lamprey, 9, 11, 22
Louis VI, 8

M
marzipan sculptures, 12

medicine, 28, 35–36
Middle Ages, 5–6, 42

N
nobles, 5, 18, 30, 32, 34

P
peasants, 5, 19, 30, 32, 34, 38, 40
Peter of Blois, 18–19
porridge, 5
pottage, 30
preserving, 26, 28–29
    brine, 29

S
scurvy, 36
servants, 13, 19
siege, 40, 42

T
table manners, 14, 15
trenchers, 14

U
utensils, 14

W
waste, 14, 16
water, 17, 40
wine, 12, 17–18, 36